D0059922

DE-ACCESSIONED

Natrona County Library
Casper, Wyoming 82601

ROS
Rosen, M.

JUN 07 2012

running with trains

running with **trains**
a novel in poetry and two voices

michael j. rosen

WORD/ONG
honesdale, pennsylvania

Text copyright © 2012 by Michael J. Rosen
All rights reserved
For information about permission to reproduce selections
from this book, contact permissions@highlights.com.

Wordsong
An Imprint of Boyds Mills Press, Inc.
815 Church Street
Honesdale, Pennsylvania 18431
Printed in the United States of America

ISBN: 978-1-59078-863-9

Library of Congress Control Number: 2011917948

First edition
Design by Barbara Grzeslo
Production by Margaret Mosomillo
The text of this book is set in Futura light, Serifa regular, and Sabon regular.

10 9 8 7 6 5 4 3 2 1

Contents

running with trains

inbound, outbound

Try and Stop Me

Aboard the *Cincinnatian*, Perry, age 13, is traveling from
one grandparent's home to the other's where his mother now
lives. It's the first day of autumn; only the ash trees are
anything but green. He is writing in a spiral notebook. On its
cover he has drawn a menacing eagle with an olive branch
in its beak. Under it, in psychedelic lettering he has written,
"1969. Time for change."

1.

If there's a window, I have to look out.
(I can't help it, except if I close my eyes,
even when I know what I'm going to see.)
Sometimes you want to be surprised by what's coming,
but sometimes you want to already know.

2.

When the train turns a corner, I see
the two rails in the distance heading toward
that point where they bend into one and the train—
with everyone aboard—should up and vanish.
But I don't. Another faraway point
appears. And I never reach that one either.

.   .   .

5

3.

My eyeballs start to flutter sideways if I watch
whatever's near the train skid into view:
postoffice,pairofflagpoles,
housewithflowerplantersmadeoftires,
mailboxspottedlikeacow,firehouse,
Harley'sBait&Tackle,cows,morecows.
The blurring becomes stripes that sail backward
and vanish even before the flags can flap.
What my eyes have to do is skip
ahead to pick out something new to see—
but even a few seconds of that, and my head
hurts: Everything that flickers past
clatters inside my cranium the way
a playing card, clothes-pinned to the frame
of a bicycle, clicks when the spokes spin.

4.

What's better is to press my face to the cool window
(it gently vibrates my cheekbones and hair)
and then spot the thing that's *futurest*
(I know that's not a word)—a silo, a sign—
and only focus on it until the engine
catches up for an instant, and then tosses
the view like a crumpled piece of paper
behind me. Things can't stay long in the future.

. . .

I pick something else and try to hold *it*
until it's gone as well. Nothing's for keeps.

5.

Every Sunday, the places we pass are the same—
or mostly—watching from the right side of the train.
And every Friday, I see the other side
of things—except in reverse—out the left.
There's never seeing straight ahead or behind.
It's always one side or the other. Not both . . .
like either you're for Peace or you're for War.
You wanted Humphrey to win or you wanted Nixon.
You either took the train or you stayed home.

6.

What *I* choose is not to look. Looking
instead at the windowpane that's this page I'm writing,
where I'm trying to slow down that racing blur
of too much thinking, too much needing to know
for sure, too much wondering *what if* and *why me*—
until it reaches the slower speed of words
where you can come to a period and stand still
for an instant, like I've just stepped off the train
at my station and I have to stand there,
suitcase tilting me left or right, passengers

shuffling to scoot around me, to scan the crowd
and find the one waving person I recognize
who's waiting to take me back into the rush.

Always Racing

Steve, age 9, is the youngest of six children. Only
one sister lives with him and their parents at home.
He spends time with the cows and his border collie. He
spends a lot more time by himself.

I never run to get somewhere first

or run to get away—I run to be fast,

to feel the gears of my legs shift into high,

to make a rushing wind that lifts my hair

and tugs the tear-water from my eyes.

I run to beat the train that cuts across

the corner of our hundred-acre farm.

I run to leap as if I really live

above the earth and, like a jet, only

need the ground to take off or to land.

I run to float an instant between my steps—

the air turned thick as water holds me up—

gliding that extra fraction of the leap

as I'm breathing faster than I'm running

. . .

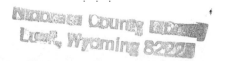

and—*thwack-smack*—my shoes slap the ground
to brake so everything stops, everything but the train
(its chugging, farther-away rhythm grows fainter)
and the beating in my eardrums that's my blood

that runs no matter that I'm stopped,
stooped over and panting. It's clanging. It's flashing
red like at a railroad crossing. It's signaling
inside of me, *I'm free, home free.*

What's Mine Is Theirs

Perry stares out the window of the half-empty coach car or
glances at the wristwatch that used to be his father's. It reads
6:05. It has read 6:05 for eleven days, ever since Perry's
fidgeting loosened the knob that winds the watch until it rolled
under his seat and disappeared.

This is *my* line, the Baltimore and Ohio,
and *my* streamliner, the *Cincinnatian*,
and *my* train, the No. 54,
that used to pull the mail container, the baggage
and the dining cars, along with the coach car
(there used to be two) where I sit in *my* seat
(closest to the window; next-to-the-last row).

But the train belongs to lots of folks: people
I never see, who board and leave before
or after me; people who suddenly ride
because a sister had a baby, or an uncle died;
people I always see—regulars like me—
they're still strangers, but I know their stops,
whether they're a window or an aisle,
whether they're a front or a back of the coach.
I know their newspapers and how they get folded,

and who brings a thermos or stewed prunes
onboard like me with my Cheez-Its and gum.
But names? No one knows mine. I don't know theirs.

Some ride to go forth, as in forward,
to a new place where they want to be happier.
Some ride to go back, as in returning,
to an old place where they know they had been happier.
And there must be others who go back and forth, like me.
Every week, like clockwork, we sit,
stationary, watching time fly
as if seconds were measured in telephone poles
or barns or cows that sail past the windows.
Tick, tick—they zip by. *Click, click,*
the wheels' lub-dub beats on the rails.

Tickets

Steve is sitting atop the fence rail along the pasture
where he's just moved the farm's cattle. He's gathered
two fistfuls of dried acorns; they're so light, even the
ones that reach the tracks barely ping. The challenge
he wishes he could try: throw a stone between the train
cars as they rumble past. He's not sure how fast his
pitch would have to be.

There is always farm work waiting for him, but
watching the train is the fuel that keeps him running.

I'm not allowed,

I know, I know, but I love to run

along the rails.

My shoes are wide as the steel,

so each foot

fits flat, balancing one

behind the other,

like I'm tracing a tightrope

stretched so high

above the ground that the train tracks

look like a zipper

ripping across the green fabric

of our pastures,

opening, closing, morning and night,

from Cincinnati
clear to the Motor City, Detroit.

I'm not allowed,
I know, I know, I KNOW! (and, yes,
my brothers knew,
we do, all of us, we know
the train schedule
like we know when the sun
rises and sets
and there's never a train or a sundown
at three P.M.!),
but I like to race on the rails
leaping over
the gravel between the wooden ties.

Your foot can't touch
or then you have to stop, go back,
and start again.
Going slow is easy, but fast?
That takes practice.

However many miles I've run
all together
they never land me farther than

where I live.
I never leave Cow Station.

Some days,
I set a penny on the rail
        and stand back
at our fence and watch the train
        roll over it,
all the wheels, car after car,
        squishing it flatter
and flatter and flatter until it's flat
        as a train ticket,
the coin stretched, and so hot—
        like the rails
right after a train passes.
        They're worth
more than a penny once they're squished:
        Kids at school
will trade things *that cost a dollar*—
        plus, they're lucky.

"Steven, you know destroying money
        is against the law."
My parents have rules for everything.
        "It's too dangerous

to play around the railroad tracks.

Go swim in the pond.

Go ride your bike. Go anywhere."

"Like ponds are *safe*?"

I argue. "And biking on winding roads?

And what about cows?

I could be trampled—except *you know*

I'm always careful."

"End of discussion," they say. "And don't

slurp through

that straw! You're only drinking noise."

But, still . . . they know.

Mom usually finds a penny

when she washes my pants.

I always carry one in my pocket—

like it's a ticket

from somewhere I really went this time.

She puts them back

in the jar that's on my nightstand.

With luck, one day,

I'll ride the train—the whole route—

not just dream it.

Home Is Where the Dog Is

Perry walks his dog along sidewalks mostly covered with
leaves that shush and crackle as they shuffle through. He thinks
of how his weeks are divided, his home life halved. Others
might feel this arrangement offers him twice as much, but they
are not Perry.

What's home to me since I have two homes now
(one with Mom and Grandpa, one with Gran),
two closets of clothes, two desks,
two beds where I sleep, two dogs,
and doubles of anything that I can't fit
in a suitcase? What's home if weekdays I'm in one place
and weekends, another: school in Wapakoneta,
then pack and travel down on the train, unpack
in Cincinnati, then travel back on the train,
borrow *this* and leave *that* behind?

Home is Homer. He's an Australian shepherd.
It's funny, I named him that when all I had
was *one* home, dog, and family
with one mom and dad, with one sister,
when "Homer" didn't hold the sound of "home."

. . .

I'm the true north of Homer's compass:
his face always sweeps in my direction.
He walks with me everywhere—leash
or no leash. His nose smears the storm door
where he watches for our car in the drive,
or the car windows when he comes for the ride.
His cloudy squiggles and dots are printed
barks we humans haven't yet deciphered.

After the letters from Dad stopped, for good,
Mom moved with Homer to live with *her* dad—
in the same room she had when she was my age,
going to school—so she could go back to school . . .
nursing school. Plus: 1.) Grandpa
grew tiny or the house grew giant
when Grandma died. 2.) Homer couldn't ride
the train with me. 3.) Homer's neck was wet
from tears. For weeks. She needed him more,
and I had to act grown-up. Like a man.
Except I wasn't. I'm not supposed to be.

Finally, Gran and I adopted a dog
for when I'm there to finish the school year:
another Australian shepherd, but more tan,
and much blacker, and almost Homer's age.
I named him Homer, too . . . Homer II.

Now, whenever I leave one home for the other,
I look out the car window, through one
Homer's smeary message and watch him watch me
drive away. Later, three hours later,
I see my other Homer watch me arrive
through his hieroglyphics on the storm door.

It's nice always being welcomed, but
I'm doubly sorry always being missed.

Homebody

Along with his border collie and the changing herd of
cows, Steve also cares for the barn cats and Lily, the one
cat who charmed her way indoors.

Our neighbor told me dogs bond with people,

but cats bond with homes. I don't know

about dogs (Nipper prefers outside

with her cows, no matter how cold or stormy the weather,

to indoors), but it's supertrue for Lily

our cat who's bonded—who's superglued—to our house.

She'll climb the wallpaper, the curtains, the window
    screens.

Sure, she likes us but I bet when she's purring

in my lap or napping between my knees on the quilt,

she's thinking, *Gee, you make a nice pillow, Mister—*

you're softer than the bookshelves . . . but not as toasty

as the TV set or sunny as the window ledge.

.   .   .

Curled up, Lily makes a pillow herself
(but you'd never want to rest your head on her),
or a paperweight for whatever you're trying to read.

She'll hardly go outside. The car is so upsetting,
she's never been away from home unless you count
the single trip she makes each year to scratch our vet.

Wedged between the alcove window and the blinds,
she welcomes the day before anyone knows it's there.
Her motor running, she's the heartbeat of home.

My Sometimes Own Room

Perry is thinking about the room in Gran's house where
he spends weeknights while at junior high. He's known most
of his classmates since kindergarten when his nickname
was Pear Bear. No one, not even his sister, can call him
that now.

Weekdays, when I stay at Gran's,
her guest bedroom becomes mine.
The floorboards groan.

The door creaks. The linen
bedspread crackles as I climb in.
If there's morning sun,

it seeps through the curtains
(like gauzy clouds, they're thin)
and warms me, wakes me from the dream I'm in.

Or if it's breezy and the window's open
the fabric will flutter across my nose and chin
until my eyelids widen,

. . .

just two slits, to prove it's not Gran
who's kissing me like when
I slept over as a little kid, and it's not Dad flown in

from training to take Annie and me fishing,
first thing, and after that, to the drive-in
for silver-dollar pancakes and bacon.

Awake, for certain,
I dress and join Gran in the kitchen,
where breakfast is ready—just one

setting—like before Dad had a son
or a wife or a house of his own—
or a war on a continent that's oceans

away where we don't belong,
even if our side can win—
and the guest room was his alone.

Snow Drafts

For Steve, shopping malls, cinemas, and sporting arenas are 30 or 45 minutes away, but when the roads aren't snowplowed, they might as well be across the continent.

Out here the snow is blank and bright like it's a letter you're supposed to write and can't think of what to say. But then, you go out in it, and your footprints are the words. It's only your first draft, but still, the steps freeze, and—too late!— you can't correct anything. Walking in your steps—from yesterday, the day before, from weeks ago—is like reading your letter: They take you back to all the places that you walked. If you fit your feet backward in the prints, they take you home. Their dotted lines map a story about you: Here's the trail to where the school bus waits, to the hay-loft and out to the feed lot, beyond the front-yard gate to the mailbox, down the road, across the neighbor's drive. The only thing is. . . snow makes as-far-as-you-can-see in-to one gigantic property that everybody must own—except nobody but your own shadow is ever around. For days, each and every time you walk, the tracks get wider . . . until, like tonight, we're expecting five to seven inches. I wish we'd have an avalanche—or such deep drifts of snow that I could build a frozen fort, where the tunnels

24

and chutes are so slick and slippery I could slide right over to . . . anywhere I wanted to go. That's something your boots could really write about! No chance. When the school bus arrives tomorrow, there will be just another page to fill up with different lines among the even deeper drifts. *Dot, dot, dot* . . . your boots pack down the snow. It's another draft of the almost exact same story, and it ends with those three periods that mean "it just *continues* . . ."

Niobrara County Library
Lusk, Wyoming 82225

Between Stations

Perry boards the train much later than usual. An ice storm hit
overnight. In brilliant sunlight, everything dazzles, even the
dullest details—power lines, telephone poles, fields of cornstalk
stubble—that never catch Perry's eye. Today is Sunday.

This mammoth church we pass always poses
questions or lectures at the train: WANT FAST,
FAST RELIEF? TAKE TWO TABLETS! —MOSES.
Its marquee towers like the mast

on an ancient ship except it's tanker size,
floating off the coast of the rails
in a sea of blacktop where cars anchor
Sunday mornings. All it's missing are sails.

CAN'T SLEEP? COUNT YOUR BLESSINGS! Or this one:
LET US HELP YOU STUDY FOR YOUR FINAL EXAM!
(Oh right, the *test* that guarantees us heaven
if we repent and say "darn" instead of "damn.")

Everything else is short between our stops
(compared to the church, at least) and doesn't preach:

stables, electric poles, towers—the top
of the train is fifteen feet . . . and its smoke might reach

to heaven, depending where that exactly starts.
But Glad Tidings is the opposite of that church:
It's hidden behind the station where Mom parks
to pick me up or drop me off. It's not much

of a ministry—more like an abandoned place
that was asked to be the chapel by all the neighbors.
At the entrance, there's a glass-doored case,
poster size, peeling paint, with words

of movable letters: THIS WEEK'S SERMON:
and then, a single word, HOPE, with space
for the rest of the subject. For months, there's just been one
sermon, the one word, HOPE, fixed in place.

Today I said goodbye to Mom, and then,
I don't know why, I walked up to the box.
It wasn't rusted shut. The door swung open.
Inside, at the bottom, along with two locks

were dozens, maybe hundreds, of plastic letters,
so someone *could* have posted other quotations—

told us what to hope for, and how to be better—
but no. It's like when we're between stations,

and the train is stuck for what feels like forever—
until we're moving again . . . as if . . . the fuel
we'd run out of was hope, and more had to be delivered.
My train was boarding. I added a *J* and a *U*

and an *S* and a *T* in front of HOPE—JUST
HOPE. Because, unless it hurts, you must.

rebound

Wait

Among Steve's first memories is being held in his
mother's arms; his feet dangle above the rain-soaked
barn floor. His father is helping a cow with a difficult
birth. The dawn light pours through the sliding door
just as the calf shimmies out. Its wet hide glistens in the
sudden light.

Steve remembers watching for a long time, thinking
that the cow was trying to lick the shine off her new calf.

At six, that calf is now the oldest cow on the farm.

Day after day, always on schedule, the trains
are like the cows that follow me from their station
inside the paddock, to the feeding pen, the barn,
one of the pastures . . . then back to the station again.
I'm the conductor. Our train has thirty cars.
And every one is a hungry dining car.

Especially in late winter or late fall,
the best thing to do, right after supper, is wait
for No. 53 as it heads from Lima
to stop in Wapakoneta at six on the dot.
And we're ten minutes—exactly midway—
between the *Cincinnatian*'s two stops.

.   .   .

I wait by the border fence. If the cows
are out, they join me there. They're not scared.
They're munching alfalfa like it's something
they're warming up to say as soon as someone
will stop talking and listen. Oh, *I* listen
even while I'm listening for the 53.

I think "moo" is just short for "moo-ve."
That's all they say to me, anyway.
*Moo-ve away. Moo-ve the gate and let us
into that pasture. No, the other one
where the grass is taller. And moo-ve that collie!*
And they listen, I think. But whatever I say

is just long for "wait." *Wait, I'll bring
you a bucket of corn. Wait, after school,
I'll open the gate. Wait and keep waiting.*
That's what animals do: They wait for us.
It's different when I'm waiting, like for the train.
I don't watch for it, don't turn my head,

or slide my gaze to the side. (Cows see that way
so they can sight a coyote that comes near.
But the only predators here are butchers.)

For sure, the cows spot the train first.
They also hear—and ignore—the whistle first,
since they hear better, and not just to the side.

So then, since it's dusk, the headlight suddenly
shines along the trees where the tracks bend.
As the train turns straight ahead, the beam
blazes down the rail . . . like it's spreading fire
or like the rails are rainbows (but only yellow)
that the train has stretched across Ohio.

Now daylight blasts back onto the trees
and fence posts, one right after another.
And my boots vibrate, my hands on the fence tremble.
There's the engine's Cyclops eye of light!
I plug my ears and squint through my lashes
as the cars whoosh past, splitting the air,

whirling crumbled leaves into tornadoes,
fluttering the yellow tags on the cows' ears,
whipping the warm train-wind across my face—
just the right side, because still, I'm staring
straight, watching what just had been day-bright
switch back to evening-dark, but darker.

. . .

If I keep staring ahead, waiting with the cows,

it will all happen again, faithfully,

but from the *left*: that would be No. 12,

rumbling through at fourteen after midnight.

Even Dad isn't up that late—or early.

No one but the conductor is watching then.

Snapshots

Shuffling among the boxes he'd helped his mother stack in
his grandpa's living room (everyone really "lives" in the den,
so no one minds), Perry opens a carton labeled Photos #3.
His mother is always saying, "One day, I'm going to sort these
into albums." She has lots and lots of "one-day" projects.
They're just not happening today.

Was I ever that little? That skinny? That tan?
Why wasn't I smiling? Why weren't we all?
What were we doing besides waiting for the flash
of the camera that signaled, *Okay, you can go!*

We were always half out the door, bundled
into snowsuits . . . dressed up for a holiday . . .
costumed . . . holding the squirming puppy . . . or posed
with cousins or teammates clutching our helmets or gloves,

finally leaving, when Dad would call, "Wait!
Picture Time!" above our protests—not
only mine, but anyone else who was present.
"One day you'll want to remember this,"

he'd say, one eye squinting closed, the other
concealed behind the camera's pirate's patch.

This? This *what?* This day in the hallway,
sourpussed (or pretending we were), stalled

between There, *where we had to get to now*,
and Here, in limbo, at home, *where we absolutely
couldn't stay another minute*, squishing
together, facing Dad, smiling, posing

as stiffly as those portraits of Mom and Dad,
and grandparents and great-aunts framed
or squeezed in albums as thick as the phone book.
So now . . . what do these remember? Maybe,

they show how hard it was for us to go—
go anywhere. But as for *where* we went
or *what* we did? That was gone in a flash.
The only thing that lingers—just like the flash

that makes you blink, then hovers a moment
before your eyes recover—are boxes of Dad's
pictures. But none of them remembers Dad.
His face was like a mirror; it doesn't see itself.

Ghost Stories

Tossing square bales from the hayloft (where he has built tunnels and a secret hideout among the stacked bales), Steve can almost picture the century of residents who have filled and refilled the farmhouse—just as the generations of cows have come and gone from their fields, although more quickly.

I make up stories about the kids who would be old by now who lived here before we did. And about the kids before them. And before them: They're probably ghosts already. Or maybe angels. An old farmhouse makes you think of them. Someone else's running feet wore down the steps I bound up to the attic. And where a kid would spy out the highest window, there's writing that someone later tried to hide with paint. The creaking swing set rusted before we started swinging here. Even though our house has lamps, electricity, and dryers, Dad says some kid like me brought coal into the bin where we store paint. Some kid tied horses to the lamppost where we've trained roses. I climb the same sour cherry-tree that was only shorter then, and before that, just a pit. The same cold spring still fills the well that someone dug as soon as these empty acres became a farm. And what about the kids who'll live here after us, after the last one of us leaves? Already my three brothers and my oldest sister have moved; I've never seen the cities where they live. Already it's too much work with just me and my sister to help. (She barely does a thing, and as soon as she goes to college in June, she'll do *nothing*!) Dad and Mom don't ever want to sell the farm. They could never live in a town with nothing to take care of. Or in an apartment . . . where you ride an elevator just to touch the earth.

I might have kids one day. Some afternoon, just to surprise them, I might pull into this driveway and point to this even older farmhouse and say, "Here's where our family lived when I was your age." And I know they won't believe me. They'll giggle. They'll shout back, "*You?* You were *never* our age," because that's what I said to Dad when he surprised me one time in the driveway of the home he loved so long ago. You might as well believe in ghosts.

On the Border

Every week, during one or another train ride, Perry writes his sister. Even when he's determined just to tell her something important, other subjects find their way into his letter. They're like stray cats: neither can you keep them all, nor can you exactly turn them away.

Dear Annie,
        I just witnessed the coolest thing:
Some farmer's cow had wandered near the tracks.
So the train suddenly slowed. This brown-and-white,
hunkered-down dog charged this huge cow

that had the same pattern of brown and white.
(The whole place looked like it had been painted
by someone who figured two colors were all
you need, like in those photographs of our great-

great-somebodies that surrounded the dinner table
as if they made our tiny family larger.)
The other cows waited in the pasture
behind the fence where they grazed, ignoring

. . .

the shouting boy—I couldn't hear him either,
though I could see him flick his arm one way,
so that the border collie ran that way,
right at the cow's heels—and the cow kicked

as he fled, but the dog had already circled again,
switching around—between the cow's legs!—
nipping, yapping, badgering the beast
until she moseyed back through the broken fence.

Maybe half a minute passed—like a fight
in the movies that's so rehearsed no one gets hurt.
I'm figuring this cow was simply tired
of shuttling back and forth between fields,

and hoped to hop a ride on the B&O—
be a boxcar cow and travel this Great Land
that stretches between Whereverville and Detroit.
By the time my window moseyed past the cow,

she was grazing next to her law-abiding buddies,
and the collie gazed at the cows like nothing
had happened, and probably wouldn't any time soon.
The last thing I could see as we gathered speed

· · ·

was the boy hammering a long white board
across the broken fence that bordered the rails.
Add some flashing lights and a clanging bell,
and he'll have his own railroad crossing!

But Annie, I keep thinking, 1.) What if
the dog had been in the house? the kid, at school?
Or 2.) What if the entire herd had followed
the one that busted out? I can just hear the conductor:

"Surprise! We've just pulled into a *new* station . . .
Watch your step as you exit the train—*and careful
of the manure.*" I bet that boy has enough acres
he never steps on the same piece of ground twice.

His grandma probably bakes him pies with apples
from trees she planted back when she was a girl.
His granddad probably whittles those life-size ducks,
telling stories of growing up there . . . by a fire

that blazes with logs the two of them chopped on Sunday.
And I bet the kid rides his own thoroughbred,
a racehorse—it's brown and white, no doubt!—
so he can gallop instead of bus to school.

. . .

Annie, I bet he never boards the train
to do a single thing; his life's right here.
Fast forward: ten or twenty years
from now I'm looking out this window

(assuming the B&O keeps running),
and there he'll be, plenty taller, for sure,
maybe bearded or married, with his border collie,
maybe his current dog's grown-up puppy,

or that dog's pup and that dog's.
Plus how many generations of cows?
(Okay, Ms. Vegetarian, you can pretend
that all his cows end up in greener pastures

instead of ground-up patties and leather belts.)
Only thing is, if we were farmers, Annie,
we'd plant cantaloupes or lima beans
or something else that we could grow—and grow

to love—but still give up without it hurting.
Cows, horses, even that chameleon
we got Dad to buy us at the fair
whose eyes could stare, one at each of us,

while you called *her* Miss Cammie from your side
of the terrarium and I called *him*
Mister Leon from mine? They all get loved.
You told me you set him loose so I could hate you—

remember?—instead of crying because a lizard died.
Maybe you're better than me at giving things up:
You boogied off to college, "Big whoop."
I didn't used to think too much about

too much. But now I do. Fast forward—
no, wait! I'd rather rewind. Speaking of,
next Sunday's their anniversary—
should have been their twenty-fifth. I can't

tell you what to do, but call—collect
even—Mom would love that. Come on, Annie,
it's just the three of us now. Save the world,
but save some time for us, okay?

                                        Love, Pair

Where I Really Want to Go

Homework finished, Steve heads out into the dusky
light with Nipper to bring in the cattle, who are already
waiting in the snow-crusted pasture just outside the corral.
It's one of those easy routines that all parties perform—
cattle, dog, and boy—almost without thinking. Which is
why Steve's concentration is often elsewhere.

I'd go anytime . . .

by plane or train or boat—I'd even row

the *Britannia* like John Fairfax

who crossed the Atlantic ocean *alone* . . .

it took him *half* of a *whole year*! . . . just him

eating, sleeping, and rowing by himself—

if I could see the World's Fair in Japan.

Right on that crowded island, I could visit

77 countries *plus* the rock

Apollo 12 brought home from the moon!

But I'd never want to go all that way alone.

I'd go anytime . . .

the supersonic Concorde jet blasts off.

I'd break the sound barrier *anytime*

to go *anywhere*! Even to Piqua,

which would probably take a single second

from our pasture-runway and two—at the most—
from anyplace in the county . . . where a grape
is going to be the only Concord you'll see.

            I'd go anywhere . . .
the Apollo flies, even Apollo 13
that exploded and had to return to Earth
and almost didn't—*but it did* . . . or anywhere
Explorer 1 flew for its 12 years—
that's three years before I became an earthling.
But I'd only go for a month, at most,
because I know I couldn't take Nipper,
or even if I could, she gets carsick,
bad! . . . and rocketsick has got to be worse.

And I'd go on any Mariner mission to Mars,
but I can wait until the voyage is quicker.
Now it takes six months to travel there, *plus*,
the only passengers on board are cameras,
and only their pictures ever return to Earth.
No, coming home has to be a part
of going away so you can tell strangers
where you're from, and then, the people who missed you,
where you've been and how you missed them, too.

Keeping Track

Perry always jots the weekly message on the Wayside Ministry's marquee in his notebook. Today it reads: GIVE THE DEVIL AN INCH, AND HE'LL BECOME THE RULER! For the first time, Perry imagines the minister looking out the church window, composing these sayings in a notebook of his own, as Perry's train crosses his view.

1. Outside the train windows, there's no news:

Cows graze as if grass will always grow that lush green.
Ducks dive as if rivers will always run sparklingly clear.
Birds fly as if wind will always blow fresh and clean.
Even cars idle at railroad crossings and tractors

crisscross cornfields as if nothing will ever change what they're doing or where they're heading.

2. Inside the train windows, there's only news:

Newspapers and magazines spread open in front of your eyes, and all the cover stories and headlines mean the same thing: *Everything's about to change. For you, too. Yes, YOU.*

We're riding the current of current events. We're swirling in a whirlwind of news from all over . . . as if a hurricane had uprooted everything—from Vietnam and Israel and Washington and Africa—and flooded together everyone's future.

. . .

3. I need to number things just to know where I am. Otherwise, life—and all the lives that are a part of mine—gets confused: I feel like too many people are telling me what to do and all at the same time.

Numbers can be anchors.

Or pushpins. The world needs to be numbered. And then, *then* it can spin.

4. There is no such thing as just coming along for the ride—even if you're not the conductor, not the pilot, not the captain, not the commander. You can be nine, thirteen, eighteen, twenty-one, fifty-five, a hundred: You can't just sit here and pretend that you're above it all and that you don't leave muddy footprints on the planet for someone else to mop up.

One paper said that 20 million Americans celebrated Earth Day and that it was the largest demonstration in U.S. history—maybe, in the history of Earth.

But still, that means 180 million Americans didn't join in.

5. Twenty million out of 200 million Americans? It's hard to feel 1/10 hopeful.

6. Because of Senator Kennedy, my sister may get to vote this year. She doesn't have to wait until she's 21. Teenagers may get the right to vote on the war they have to fight in.

. . .

7. If his law passes, then I can vote in five years. And fight.

I can fight like Dad fought. And if I end up missing like Dad is missing, maybe I'll find him. There. Wherever that is. That place where we all will find ourselves some day.

How old do you need to be NOT to fight?

8. In Sunday's paper, the "Ripley's Believe It or Not" cartoon featured a man with the world's longest fingernails, a woman with skin like an alligator, and an eight-foot clock carved with a pocket knife from a single pine tree. I think the whole world fits in the "believe it or not" category. Most times, I want to pick "or not."

9. Maybe outside the train, like on the farms we're barreling past, the news only happens on the acres you have. Maybe that's all you need: the duties, the relatives and neighbors, the damages that weather and whatever else brings. Maybe if I lived here, out here, off the beaten track—off the *train* track, like on that farm where the kid with the border collie lives—things would be different.

10. Or not.

11.

Where I'd Never Go

Sunday evening, his parents make time for an
hour-long news program on the television, after
which Steve checks on the two cows who are ready
to give birth any moment and continues the travel
reverie he began earlier.

I'd never go . . .
to Biafra in Africa, or anywhere
where kids have bellies that bulge like they're full—
but they're empty . . . like a balloon on a stick.
Almost every magazine at school
features a full-page picture of their famine.
Our grade donated money. It wasn't so much.

I'd never go . . .
to Mississippi where that hurricane . . .
or Lubbock, Texas, where that huge tornado . . .
or Peru, where earthquakes and landslides
swept away thousands and thousands of people . . .
or the shores of California, where the oil rig
spilled zillions of gallons for hundreds of miles
and tarred the beaches and suffocated dolphins
and poisoned and drowned the seabirds or gave them
    pneumonia.

49

.   .   .

Not going . . .
to the Middle East where every country
wants the same thing: everything.

I'd also never go anywhere . . .
in a car that's called a Gremlin. It's $2,000,
and we're not rich, I know, but it's a spazzed-out,
sawed-off station wagon! Dad decided
on "Grasshopper Green." He thought that was funny
since grasshoppers already park at our farm.
But the car itself is the joke! Mom won out:
the car's "Snow White"—so now it's a fairy tale
for little kiddies, *plus* a joke. I can walk.

Even though it's only in Ohio, I'd never go . . .
to the Cuyahoga River that's so polluted
it *caught on fire*: a smoking river of flames
that flows to Cleveland where there's smoke from riots
like in Harlem, Chicago, Atlanta, Detroit—
I don't want to go anywhere we discuss
in Current Events. Anti-war protests,
Flower Power, Black Power, the shooting
at Kent State—that's Ohio, too.
Maybe if you'd already visited those places,
you'd know the one where you could really help.

. . .

What if the places I don't want to go become
so many there won't be anywhere else but here?

Neck **and Neck**

Steve and Nipper have been wandering their forested acres, unsuccessful so far, in their hunt for this one kind of mushroom that isn't poisonous (still, he doesn't like the taste), which his mother fries up with eggs for breakfast. They've just emerged from the woods.

Perry has covered several pages of his notebook with alphabets he's inventing. One has flowers inside the opening of letters like O and P. Another is puffy letters, scalloped like cumulus clouds. In the various styles he prints, "It's not a problem if money can fix it." It's one of the sayings Gran's fond of sharing. He looks up to see the sky is suddenly sunny.

That farm kid's really racing our train?
At least, for this second, we're neck and neck.
But once we reach 45 miles per hour?

I know every car that's ever been coupled
on the Baltimore and Ohio:
diner, sleeper, fridge car, flat car, box car,
tank car, cattle car, mail car, post office,
fiesta car, engine, and last, caboose.
I rattle off a name each time my foot
hits ground, and then I run, saying them faster
and faster until the syllables streak together,
and I can't breathe enough for all the words

blasting from my mouth. If words were gray
as you spit them out, they'd be the chimney smoke
from an old steam engine streaming straight behind me.

He can't have been running since . . . Wapakoneta?
Was that his starting block? Did he just hurtle
those fences, wade that rocky stream, weave
among the muddy ruts of the tilled fields?
Now he's braking, jamming his shoes to stop,
bending in half to catch his breath—and grinning!
And waving . . . good-bye probably—maybe
he's got a brother heading to the Peace Corps;
maybe, a dad who's in the ROTC?
I wave back as if I were the conductor
motioning to hurry, we're about to depart.

That teenager—is he waving at me?
He looks so serious in the window . . . like he's looking
for someone who was supposed to meet him at the station
but didn't show up. Or maybe he's only wiping
the fog of his close-up breathing from the view.

So, which of the eleven passengers
is the one he's going to miss? It's not me . . .
You can't outrun a train. No reason you can't try.

Commemorative Stamps

Perry has tucked a dozen stamped envelopes into the
pocket of his notebook's back cover. Each one is
addressed to his sister.

Dear Annie,

        Have I told you I've been to Cairo?
Dozens of times! Our train just pulled in now.
And Egypt's here in Ohio, too! I read this
in a magazine a lady left on the seat:
some pioneer decided that "Egypt" was perfect for—
and this is a quote—this "dab of mud that fell
from the wheelbarrow of God when He made the world."
(The Garden of Eden had a real gardener?
One that mucked around in coveralls
and boots like a plain old farmer?)
So far, no sign of pyramids.

It's weird how the whole world found
its way to Ohio. There's London, Athens,
Toronto, Dublin, Holland, Poland, Peru.
Founding fathers from all over, I guess,
wanted to feel their homelands had arrived

along with their steamer trunks in America.
If so, then where'd the folks come from who founded
Spanker, or Knockemstiff, Spunky Puddle,
Pigtown, Pigeye, or Ratsville? They're all on our map!

Remember when I used to collect stamps
with Dad? I mean, remember when Dad gave me
the stamp collection he started as a boy
and hoped that I'd continue instead of just making fun
of far-off, *far-out* lands like Madagascar
or Chad, who gets a whole country for himself?
The only stamps I would have added were his,
the ones that should have come from Vietnam.
But all his letters arrived with just "FREE,"
in his handwriting, where the stamp would go.
I didn't need to steam the envelope
to loosen that, the way he showed me for stamps.
I snipped the word FREE . . . it was sometimes blue,
sometimes black, and always all capitals . . .
from every envelope and slid them in the slots
so every row on every page chanted
"FREE, FREE, FREE, FREE, FREE."
Then the letters stopped. Remember how
every time we opened the mailbox
we couldn't help thinking—

. . .
                            I'll change the subject.
Remember when I used to make commemorative stamps
for the dumbest things, for just anything
we did. Remember that lake we tried to fish
where water snakes kept swimming past our canoe
and we almost capsized from everybody lurching—
well, not Dad—to the opposite side of the boat?
Remember, our backyard campouts or bingo with Gran,
or when we watched dollars being printed
at the Mint and hammered crabs for lunch on the bay?
Remember, I'd draw up postage stamps and snip
a jagged edge with those creaky pinking shears?
Maybe I'll design some stamps for all
these foreign lands stranded here in Ohio.

I've always wondered how the post office
decides on who or what deserves a stamp.
I have a 6-cent stamp of Apollo 8.
And Grandma Moses. And John Wesley Powell
who must have done something a hundred years ago—
something in a canoe—that we can celebrate
with postage. Whoopee! Let's lick his stamp!
And then I still have a sheet of stamps,
"Search for Peace" (the dove with the olive branch),
from the year Dad's letters . . . I'll change the subject.

. . .

How about the subject of why I never
get letters from you? I'll even send you the stamps.
For FREE. Or is "Stamp Out Letters!" another
of your protests? "Give peace a chance!" Great.
But how about giving your brother a chance?
Or Mom? Doesn't free love mean you've got
lots to spend? Isn't your world bigger
than you, Annie? I hope you're happy, and that
happiness is all you need.

                          Pair

Belonging

Collecting snail shells that washed up on the farm
pond's bank, Steve fills a giant olive jar that his uncle
Eric, who owns a pizza shop, saved for him.

My uncle always calls me a keeper, and smiles,

because he's a letter-go. When we fish

for carp, I want to keep them, just for a while,

in our wading pool. I save cocoons and wish

they'll hatch, there on our sill. "A living thing

belongs right where you found it." He shrugs. "Outside

things should stay outside. What good's collecting?"

Birds' nests, a crawdad shell that's dried,

a papery hive, fossils, a skeleton—

I've made a nature center in our den.

I caught a praying mantis once in a jar.

"Now what? Most fool thing you've kept by far!"

my uncle scolded. "No, honest, I'm setting it free.

But I had to bring it home for you to see."

Everyone Has a Point of View

A mother and daughter are arguing in whispers in the seat
behind Perry. He tries not to listen, but he can't help it, just
as he can't help thinking about the return trip even before he's
arrived. They both go back and forth over the same ground.
It all reminds Perry of something Gran says: "A dog will
scratch his fleas in the kennel, but not on the hunt."

Across the cabin, my view is newspapers
stretched between other passengers' hands.
They don't see anything through the windows
behind me. They don't see me. I don't see them.

I don't see anything through the windows
behind them. On *their* side of the papers,
the headlines and photos and comics and ads
compose their view. *My* side stays the same.

When someone walks past, the pages flutter,
just a little, like a bedsheet the breeze
rustles on a laundry line—like a flag
the train's gusts ruffle in our draft.

When someone turns a page, their hands clap,
but softly, almost like when you pray,

and the paper shuts like a butterfly's wings,
becoming, for just that moment, a single line,

as if all the news turned into just one headline
announcing . . . that love had finally made peace
in the world or that war or air pollution
or overpopulation had finally made . . .

the final edition—nothing left to report.
But in that same instant, the view reappears
in the train windows behind that thin headline:
the rushing smear of orchards, pastures, barns,

school yards, traffic . . . strangers sweeping or shopping
whether the latest news was better or worse
than feared. And then the pages spread open—
another beat of the wings—and what's changed?

Future

Steve's eyes are headlights that follow the craze of lines
that run across the old paint on his bedroom ceiling.
It's like his world is upside down: He's in clouds of
pillows, looking down on all the streams and streets that
intersect. Then a crack of lightning—another jagged
track—sets things right again.

Behind each window shade that's drawn I bet
there's a passenger who's dozing so the dawn
blurs into afternoon and then the dusk.
All those daydreams probably sail up to the clouds
with the engine's exhaust. And when the passengers
awake, they're suddenly in a different place!
It's like they all were dreaming of this destination
and when they arrived, that dream came true.

Planting- or harvest-nights when someone's working
the bigger tractor, its two beams travel
the bedroom ceiling. I lie there, pretending
it's the B&O, it's the locomotive's light
reflecting on the two bright rails running
across the route that's mapped among the paint's
cracks and spots. I could be the conductor.
(I can already drive the tractor—if they'd let me.)

. . .

And when the wheels slow in a hairpin turn

closest to the house and the lights disappear,

I can feel the train—it's not a dream at all:

The headboard rumbles just like when I'm standing

at our fence and it rattles as the cars

hurtle past as fast as time passing

when you're asleep and then it's the next day.

A train takes you straight into the future.

A tractor . . . it just runs back and forth, like before.

How Can Something Be True If Its Opposite Is Also True?

Awakened by his mother fumbling in the closet as she left for a late shift at the hospital, Perry gives up trying to fall back asleep. He flips to the next empty page in his notebook, and begins to number his thoughts.

1. Fact: It's selfish of someone (Mom, for instance) to move us to another city so she can go to school, when someone else (me, for instance) is still at the school where we used to live.

The opposite: It's selfish for the other person (that's me) to want something that means someone else (that's Mom) can't have what she says will provide for what we all need (that's me, my sister, and Mom). That's three selves winning, instead of just one self.

We need a lot of things.

2. Another fact: Everyone is selfish: We're each just one person trying hard to be happy.

The opposite: Nobody is selfish: Different people sometimes want different things that can't both happen, like a coin landing heads *and* tails—or on its edge. (I'd like to see that.)

3. Fact: When two peoples (countries, for instance) want different things that can't both happen, you have war. And then people (Dad, for instance) have no choice. They can't be selfish even if they want to be.

Back to 2. Instead of happy, some people try hard to be powerful.

4. Fact: Every day, my mother wears a pendant with a drawing of a sunflower. Among the leaves, the words read: "War is not healthy for children and other living things." Once the war ends, she says she'll put it away in a drawer. For good.

Love is the opposite of war. Every day, she wears her engagement ring and her wedding ring—they clasp into a single ring, like a husband and wife in a marriage, she says. Once my older sister marries someone, Mom will give her the rings.

She's already given me Dad's silver cat's-eye cufflinks—they're green.

Dad's eyes were green like the cufflinks.

No one inherited his eyes. No one has shirts that need cufflinks.

5. A fact about my sister in college that's the opposite: She says she'll *never* get married because that would be giving in to our oppressive society. She is studying to be a free spirit who will live on a commune where everyone's in love with everyone and

everyone wears psychedelic T-shirts they tie-dyed themselves and writes poems without capital letters and really long folk songs to perform at coffeehouses that are even smokier than the coach car when it used to be full.

She also believes marriage would only stifle her because, along with taking classes to be a social worker, she's busy crafting rainbow candles so she can open a shop with her friend Sunshine, who used to be her friend Cynthia, who creates far-out jewelry with beads and shells. The last time I saw my sister she looked like a cross between my braces and a coral reef.

In addition, she's going to attend Yale so she can become a sandal-wearing, sandalwood-smelling hippie lawyer once she's helped some disadvantaged children and sold a gazillion candles.

I don't know if my sister is radically selfish, really selfish, or just the regular selfish that I was wondering about earlier.

6. Wanting peace isn't selfish. It might be the opposite.

7. A fact and its opposite: Mother's counselor told her that people are in charge of their own happiness. But then Mother told me that if a child is unhappy, how can the mother be anything but unhappy, since a child's happiness makes a mother happy?

It would be selfish to make my mother unhappy.

. . .

8. A fact: I am not a self trying hard to be unhappy. But "happy" can be such a stupid word. Puppies make you happy? Okay! You cover your refrigerator with pictures of them. But do they make you "happy" when you find their poop caked on your sneakers or when they've chewed a library book that costs you $18 to replace?

9. A fact: I should go to bed. The end.

10. Its opposite: I'll never fall asleep now. This is not all I have to write on the subject because, guess what? I'm not even sure what the subject is. The counselor who told Mother to keep a journal said the whole point is *not* to stick to the subject. Let the topics flow! Don't try to tie up loose ends. You're always going to think of something else that's going to be number 11.

11. When the war is over, sure, some things will end, but people continue, and they'll be people-who-survived-a-war. They're not the same even if they stayed home and only read about the war. Or tried not to.

     And when people die in a war, sure, their bodies end but other things about them continue. They reappear in your home movies and photographs—even in the ones they're not in because they probably held the snapshot you're holding in your hand. You hear their voice in the nickname you wouldn't answer to except for them, or when you retell their favorite joke about

the priest, the minister, and the rabbi stranded on a desert island that's now your favorite. You may see them when you look in your mirror even if your eyes are more like a bluish gray.

12. Mom is not supposed to number her journal thoughts, but I do. Numbers are like the street signs and mile markers you see from the train that let you know you're not just running in a loop like the model train in the Cub Scout troop leader's basement.

No one is telling me to keep a journal.

This isn't a journal. It's just where I think in private.

I don't even want to share this book with *me*. I don't look back at what I wrote down yesterday or six months ago. Maybe one day I will.

I doubt it.

13. A fact: If I were wearing a shirt that had cufflink slots I think the only subject to write about would be the dad's-eye cufflinks staring back at me like he was waiting for my answer.

Its opposite: I wish there were one.

Kitchen Rules

After another week of spring rains that turned the
corral into a slurry of manure and mud that sucked a
boot off his foot not once, but four times, landing him
twice on his knees, Steve wasn't in the mood for a
lecture because he broke the rule about starting dinner
before everyone was seated. Or for telling a grown-up
that you don't want to be lectured.

Do not play with your food. That's why we bought you
    games.

Food stays in the kitchen. Popsicles count as food.

Do not just stand there with the refrigerator open.

Do not drink milk from the jug. That's why we bought
    glasses.

Try not to make that *glug-glug* sound when you gulp.

You can go back outside only if you've finished supper.

Popsicles do not count as supper. Or as breakfast.

What we serve is what you're having . . . we don't have
    menus.

The tablecloth is not your napkin. Nor is your sleeve.

Your knife and fork are not for drumming on the table.

You can't have two desserts. That's what tomorrow is for.

Yes, we know that glasses make different pinging
    sounds

when hit, and we know where headaches come from,
     don't we?
Ignore the dog. She'll stop begging when you stop sharing.
Never show anyone the food that's in your mouth.
Ignore your cousin when he says he really wants to see it.
Do not rest your head on the table. That's what your bed
     is for.
What do you mean? Of course, there are rules about
     bedtime.
You don't think we're making all this up for fun?

Peace

During the week, Perry pushpinned some snapshots he'd
borrowed from the unsorted boxes. They're arranged into a
peace sign on the corkboard wall in his bedroom at Gran's.

Dear Annie,
         Riding this same train
drums the same few things inside my head,
like my brain runs the same two rails
but needs to get elsewhere, a place that's not
a real destination. Like about Dad.

You stay in one place, your college dorm,
so how many times a day do you think of him?
Every hour? Not every minute, do you?
You knew him five more years than me. I mean . . .
I remember him, maybe, starting at three—

that's only seven years before he left.
You want to know where I wish this train would stop?
(The war, I know, won't stop. Who's winning?
North or South, everyone loses, right?)
At the station—there has to be one—Peace,

that's not just a stop but an end.
Who has to fall asleep so that this train
of events can veer off the rails and land us there,
like here, at this farm we're rushing past
where no one's crops are burning, no one's church

is hiding hostages or wounded soldiers?
This train circles the planet. We've all boarded.
We're speeding out of control, grabbing onto
anything we can just to stop,
to stand still: You're holding those years

of Dad alive; but me? mostly I'm stuck
holding on to his dying over there.
That's the train I keep riding—writing—
rewriting to make peace with it all.
And, I know, I'm what has to give.

I know, Annie. I have to learn to live
with facts that aren't about to change or change
back. If a train of thought is really a train . . .
why can't the conductor—that's got to be me?—
control the switching yard in my head? We're here.

. . .

So what about you? Write me.

Love, P

P.S. I came across a snapshot you'd like:

Ocean City. 1958.

Dad is buried in sand and you're straddling him.

Holding me, Mom must have snapped the picture.

If Summer Were a Planet

As he finishes blasting the mud-plastered tires of two
bicycles with his sometimes ray gun, sometimes hose,
Steve invents a game—another world—with a visiting
cousin and Nipper.

If I twist the nozzle of the garden hose

just right it sprays a rainbow

inside our yard so we can trade off

holding the hose or else leaping

like grasshoppers or horses under

or over the misty rainbows that land

right on Earth, right on our farm . . .

and we are these rainbow giants

who voyaged in a rainbow spaceship

for a vacation to this planet

where we wear swimming suits all day

and picnic every meal and dive

at the pond and pick warm cherries

and stay until the lightning bugs

start their coded messages—

they're flashes to the Milky Way,

all the way from our rainbow-colored

home planet where we aren't giants,

at all, just kids, regular-size—

which we have to decode to know our mission,

to know what we have to—*what? What!*

Aw, Dad! Do we have to?—have to

coil the hose beside the pump,

and come inside the house and change.

unbound

The One That Got Away

> Mucking out the barn isn't the most pleasant work.
> It's shovel after shovel of manure dumped into a
> wheelbarrow and carted out to a mound where it can
> dry in the sun for a year or so before being spread on the
> pastures that grow the alfalfa that feeds the cows again.
> It's a cycle. Exhausted, Steve begins the task even before
> his father arrives home, changes out of his city clothes,
> and joins him. Even before his mother, who volunteers
> at the Red Cross in Wapakoneta, pulls in with the
> week's groceries.

The sequence of the afternoon's events
circles like train cars, one after another,
on the track inside Steve's head.
He wanted to tell his father, explain what happened,
but even history from an hour earlier was turning
into a half-remembered story, a wishful
tale of what never happened, but should have.

Hey, Number 10, what I don't get is:
The grass isn't greener on the other side
of the fence—it's weeds, Queen Anne's lace, spikes
and brambles . . . while here, there's sweet alfalfa
we sow and mow and rake and bale and store . . .
we even serve you in the barn come wintertime

when the grass dies back: You get breakfast in bed!
So what's outside that you want? Are you dreaming
of that first grass of spring before we mow
that must be somewhere the Cincinnatian runs?
(Do you cows dream . . . at all? The way we do?)
I hate to tell you, Number 10, but you only
get a one-way ticket on a cattle car.

Steve barely lifted his gaze from the shovel
when the narrow shadow of a head, shoulders,
and then a waving arm stretched across
the barn floor, even when the fluttering rooster
leaped across it, pursued by the collie—
one pretending to peck, the other, to herd—
enacting the daily truce they'd established
long ago.

"What kind of a greeting is that?"

"I didn't see—I mean, I was waiting
until you—"

"Too late. A father has to ask
for a 'hello'?—what's got into you?
You bathed Nipper, but your homework's splayed

across the kitchen table. And you left the hose
uncoiled on the porch where someone could trip over it . . .
so you could get a head start out here?"

"Dad, I have to tell you . . . something bad,
that wasn't my fault, but everybody blamed me."
Steve blotted a tear with a clean edge
of his sleeve and tried to clear the frog in his throat.

"Who's 'everybody'? Mom isn't even home."

"The cows broke out—where they broke out before.
But this time . . . the train—they stopped it. For an
    hour—"

"An hour? It's a ten-minute walk to the tracks . . ."

"The whistle blasted so many times. I didn't think
that it had anything to do with the herd.
Not at first. That's why it took so long.

"It's not as if *I* stopped it Dad! It's me—
Nipper and me—who got *it started* again!
Okay, it *was* our cows . . . but I wasn't doing
something else when I should have been there.

I ran till all my breath was gone, and then
I ran again—and more! It wasn't my fault . . .

"The conductor was howling at me, blaming me
even after Nipper and I began.
I was shouting commands, shouting at cows—
I couldn't figure out what command to call—
what direction to send her. It's not my fault
alone the cows broke through the broken fence again."

"What wasn't? Responsibility isn't
something you pass like a hot potato.
That's a different story. Finish this one—
No, let's just finish mucking out this stall;
you can explain when you're not so upset."

Without their voices, silence (the occasional
cooing of doves, chit-chit of swallows,
moos and snorts of cows) hung like the scent
of manure—so familiar, it's hardly even noticed.
The truth, the plain facts about the incident—
along with the only witnesses to tell it—
slipped further into wishful thinking.

Here's what should have happened: "Move those cows!"
The train conductor yells. His arms stretch out

as if he wants to be a scarecrow.
I shout back: "What do you think we're doing?
You really believe we broke the pasture fence
so we could stop your train . . . for five whole minutes?"
That's all it's going to take to round them up.
Number 10 and thirty girlfriends
are grazing right outside the span of fence
she'd broken before. "You're holding up the train."
He's not a scarecrow, he's scared, and won't come closer.

Nipper zips around her girls. "Cast,"
I call. Zigzagging, she gathers the group.
Then "Bye," and Nipper zooms left.
And then "Away": She flies around to the right.
She's giving them the eye—now that's scary,
to cows, at least. She's barking, nipping stragglers.
And see? The herd wants nothing but to be back—
like it's us—we've got the sweetest grass!

And that's it for this week's exciting
episode on the farm. It's over.
Nipper rushes the pokiest (Number 10, of course),
I pound a two-by-four across the gap,
and the conductor shouts again: "Young man!"
His voice is loud, but he's just trying to be heard
this time. "Come over to the train. And bring your dog."

. . .

The cabin is empty, except for this one boy.
At first, I guess it's the conductor's son.
Or someone famous who gets the Cincinnatian
all to himself? Then the conductor (the badge
on his uniform says YORK)—*greets him.*
"Perry, I want you to meet Steve and Nipper;
they saved the day. A little late, but still . . ."
I shake his hand, forgetting how dirty
my hand is. Except for a smear of ink,
his skin is smooth and clean as his silver watch.
Hands like that would never touch a cow.
Maybe a dog. He squats to pet Nipper
and fishes out a cracker from his jacket.

Mr. York, he says, "It's lucky, you know,
that we're on a bend as we pass his farm,
otherwise, at full speed, we'd need
half a mile for the brakes to halt this train."
(I already know that fact; I read it once
in a library book on trains I had to buy
when Nipper chewed the cover as a puppy.)
"Why don't you give Steve a tour, Perry,
while I fill out the incident report."

. . .

Perry shows me how the seats recline,
and where you tuck your ticket after it's punched,
and how the door unlatches. "Here's where
we can escape when the car is full of smokers."
Perry knows a lot about the train.
He's studied about the B&O like me.
He's saved his allowances and now he's traveling
all across the country on every line.
So we stand next to the coupling between the cars—
Nipper can't believe the train lets her
go outdoors between two indoors!—
and I pretend we're moving and we're allowed
to be outside—the whole trip!—watching
the ties flash beneath the train faster
than the second hand on his watch—maybe six
every second? And then faster and faster.

After the tour, we look out the coach-car windows
and I point out our barn—it's gigantic—
but it can hide under my finger that touches
the pane. My blurry fingerprint stays behind.
It's going to travel on the Cincinnatian.

"Are you saving up for a cross-country ticket?"
Perry may know trains, but farming? No way.

"I don't have time," I tell him. "It's only me,
really, who has to help with calving or plowing
or fixing fences or whatever else.
Plus I don't know where I'd go, Perry—
outside Ohio—where someone I know would be
waiting at the platform to meet me.
Here, or pretty nearby, is where the people
I know are, except for my twin uncles—
they've been stationed in 'Nam since January."
I pull a lucky penny out of my pocket.
"This is the only ticket I ever have,"
I drop it into Perry's hand. "You can keep it."
Then he was supposed to say, "It's really a penny?
For keeps? The train stretched it flat like this?"
And then I say, "Where'd you come from . . . Mars?
Of course, the train squished it. Don't you ever
get off the train and see what's on the ground?"

But the whistle blows. The floor begins to jiggle
as the engine fires up. I climb down with—

"An hour?"

Though softly spoken, his father's words startle
like the clang of the dinner bell, calling
Steve back.

. . .

"I'm just surprised. You've worked
those cows, all by yourself, since—"

"But never *outside* the property, Dad!
Never *all of them*! Not by *myself*!"

"All the cows—you're saying they all escaped?"

The shovel in Steve's gloved hands abruptly
stopped as if it had hit upon something
buried and heavy. *Dad. Doesn't. Understand.
Just like the conductor didn't understand
a thousand-pound cow goes wherever,
whenever she wants.* "Not just Number 10
and her usual gang, it was all the numbers,
except the penned bull and the sick calf
inside the barn."

"That 10 . . . her days are numbered."

"I got confused, and I confused Nipper.
And the cows were, for sure. If you'd been there—"

"I would have been confused. That's not a job
for one . . . one man . . . or one boy and a dog."

. . .

"But *you'd* know what to do. And Nipper, she listens
to you. A lot better than I do."

Steve's father laughed, which made Steve smile,
and then the conversation was taken up
by the two shovels, the squishing sounds of scooping
manure, the thudding splat as it dumped from the blade.

"Hungry? The rest of this can wait for the weekend."

So in the end, the way it was supposed
to happen really did. I brushed Nipper.
I bounded up the stairs—only touching
every other step. I showered and changed.
I could smell the sizzling onions, the toasty
oven rolls, and—steaks. T-bones!
That's company food—but it's just the four of us
and Nipper's already beelined to her corner.
"Okay," I say, and she gobbles a mouthful
even before the bowl touches the floor.

Peent, peent, *the nighthawks are nabbing their*
skeeter supper by the time I finish
telling Mom and Dad the story—the one
that shouldn't have happened that way but really did—

and so I ask to be excused and run out
with Nipper, and we rocket through the pastures,
soaring through the twinkling Milky Way,
gliding among the cloudy, mooing moons,
and then, grass-stained, dripping sweat,
and breathing like my space suit's tank
of oxygen was almost all used up,
splash down in the bathtub and head to bed
so I can be up early tomorrow, like always.

That Point of No Return

> In a sky that's bluer than it's been in weeks, the clouds are
> so fluffy they strike Perry as silly. They're a herd of
> marshmallow cows that floated into the atmosphere. Perry
> recalls a sky like this when his family, the four of them, lay
> on the grass, deciding what the shape of each cloud
> resembled. His father, who always seemed to know the
> oddest things, said that what they were doing actually had
> a name: nephelococcygia. Perry can't recall exactly how
> his father pronounced it, so he never gets the spelling close
> enough to find the word whenever he looks it up.

Dear Annie,

This might be my last letter

from the train. The conductor, Mr. York

(first name might be New), told me

the B&O is likely going broke.

Could be a month. Could last a year.

We had a longer talk today because,

for three stops, the only passenger

was me—and come June, *I* won't be riding.

Yes, your "little brother" . . . in high school.

And living with Mom again, wherever she moves.

Remember that cow that almost stopped the train?

(You at least *read* my letters, don't you?) Today,

she and the rest of her herd, they busted out.
At first, I figured the train whistle had broken—
I'd never heard so many blasts in a row.
Then the brakes screeched, but we were nowhere
near a station. I couldn't see the trouble
from any window until, rounding the bend,
we slowed to a total halt. And there they were:
must have been forty, fifty cows at least—
congregating between the pasture and the rails.

We probably sat there for ten minutes, idling . . .
either hoping the cows would eventually cross,
or the farm police (is there such a thing?)
would come arrest them. Finally, this farm kid
and his collie appear, so the conductor hopped out—
he said I had to stay onboard . . . some law—
just as the dog circled behind the cows.
The kid called and gestured while Mr. York
hollered and clapped. The collie, let alone
the cows, ignored him. I couldn't hear, so when
the herd turned—almost like a school
of cowfish swerving behind the glass
aquarium of the train—I couldn't say
what MOOved them first toward home, and then away.
Maybe the conductor spooked an influential cow.
They stampeded across the tracks—the stones

between the rails springing among their ankles
like sooty hail—as they scattered in all directions
(like that was one direction they *could* follow).

The kid, as well, seemed to be everywhere
at once, calling to the dog, crouching
to catch his breath, and barking, himself, at the cows.
The border collie frantically chased one pair
toward their farm . . . while others sauntered away
or stood still as if waiting their turn.
I don't know why: It somehow reminded me
of when Dad would clip my hair. He'd cut one side
but then the other would end up a tad shorter,
so he'd trim the first side to match it,
and I'd be bald, or practically, and hating him.
(Lucky you, you simply grew your hair
until you could sit on it. Lucky, except for the night,
Rapunzel, your braid caught in the revolving doors
outside the airport and we almost missed our plane.)

When the engineer jumped off the train, I joined him.
I'd forgotten how rainy the last week had been,
so hiking across the overgrown field—
all rabbit holes and puddles camouflaged
by matted weeds—my shoes flooded with sludge.

· · ·

Four cows were back where they belonged. The rest . . .
it was a lost cause. The kid cried—
shouting-crying, but maybe crying-with-tears.
Mr. York, the dog: yipping, yelling, yapping!
The cows bawled or bleated—I don't know
what it's called, but they didn't just moo.
Maybe they MOO-HOOED? The engineer
met up with the kid. Heads shook no. Then yes.

I forget, Annie, were you there when we drove
to that one petting zoo—ponies, goats,
and that pretend cow where you could sit
and tug these rubber udders and squirt milk,
pinging and splashing into a tin pail?
That was as close as I'd ever been to a cow—
until this afternoon. They kick. They run
faster than you'd guess. They stink like the sack
that holds the mower's mashed-up lawn clippings
and the sweaty insides of a baseball glove and farts.
Their golf-ball-size eyes stare right at you.

The kid who owned the cows and the collie
said his name was Steve. I'd seen him before,
running beside the train. He was drenched
from circling the cows. Maybe he was ten,
more likely eight, and *he* was giving the orders

to the three of us. Grabbing the longest branches
we could find, two on each side, we formed
a border around the cows. Raging bulls?
Charging rhinos? No—but Annie, they're massive,
and there we were amid a mob of them!

We were supposed to holler, whack the ground,
and fan the branches to form a chute that narrows
and bunches the cows together while the collie
leaped and swerved and darted among the herd
and Steve called "bye" and "hello" or whatever
so the dog knew what to do. *We* didn't know
what we were doing. Did the kid know?
That dog knew. Nipper. That we could see.

Obviously we managed to pen the cows,
and your brother was not stomped or squished flat
as this letter that you're now holding.
So Steve and his collie followed us to the train
like he was going to reboard as well,
like he wanted to say something, or expected
one of us to. Spattered with mud and manure
in every shade of brown, he was as dirty as the dog
whose patches of white were utterly hidden, whose tongue
was the only light color besides the same

white in both of their eyes. Bright pink,
it panted so rapidly I wondered if his heart
was pumping at that same exhausted rate.

I remembered I had one of Homer's treats
in my jacket pocket, so I tossed it to the collie.
It landed right beside his front paws.
The dog sniffed it and gazed up at Steve
who said, "OKAY," and *then*, he wolfed it down.
The dog was actually waiting for his signal.
Like either Homer would do that—or have to!
What kind of life is that where someone orders
every move you make: GO LEFT. GO RIGHT.
GO BACK. GO HOME. OKAY, NOW TAKE THE TREAT.

The two of them, they kept watching the train
(I know, because I kept watching them)
until we each disappeared from sight.

Annie, I know: I've written pages and pages—
and you only get the ones I put in the mail—
of what I'm going through, but at least *I'm going.*
I'm not like this kid Steve who's stuck in the mud,
who's penned in—along with his dog and cows.
(And even his cows want out!) So I know it:

I'm lucky, in *some* ways. (In *other ways* . . .?)
But thinking about luck is like worrying.
Gran is always saying: "You have something
that needs worrying about? Give it to me—
a grandmother has nothing better to do."
You'd get a hoot out of hanging with Gran.
You both talk like you have answers for it all.

And I talk like all I have are questions.
I certainly *don't* have a house. Even that Steve
might feel lucky compared to me. And, no,
two grandparents' houses don't count.
But, guess what? I do have a home
wherever a Homer is, where Mom is
and Grandpa, or Gran who's like my weekday mom,
and where you are, if you decide to come down
from your high horse on your hippie carousel
and love the family you left. We're all the family
you *have* left, Annie.

So, believe it
or not, this is my last letter to you
from the B&O. Or from anywhere.
I don't know why I kept writing you.
You're my sister. I love you. I always will.
But I can't keep sending letters like now it's *you*

who's missing in action. Dad—that was different.
We *all* kept writing. But I was dumb and young
—and so what!—I didn't pretend I was brave:
Whenever the news said prisoners were found and freed
I wrote another letter. I didn't show Mom.
For the too-longest time, I'd picture Dad
reading my letter (just like I picture you),
and writing a letter back. And then, I'd picture
a prison guard shredding his envelope
and hurling this confetti over Dad . . .
every tiny piece with the word FREE.
Or his next letter to me: burned or stabbed
or stuck on barbed wire for target practice.
I finally got it through my thick head
that it was worse to hope than to give up hope.

But with you—I can't even picture *your* letters—
it's worse to waste my time on you UNTIL
YOU decide that family isn't a waste
of your time. Writing you stirs up too much,
muddies everything—it's my own fault.

End of sermon. Feel free to resume
whatever peace you were celebrating
before I disturbed it (as if I really did?),
and I'll go back to mine. For now, it's true,

mine is riding on a train that rocks,
rumbles, wails. Remember the ocean in a bottle
you made me the Christmas after Dad left,
not for practice but for . . . forever?
That giant, empty soda container you filled—
half oil, half blue-tinted water.
I'd heave it, lifting one end, the other,
sloshing the blue into a crescendo of waves
that crashed inside that miniature water-world.
It was like our cloud-gazing, except there weren't
shapes to call out of the clear and the blue.
Instead, I shook up hurricanes and floods.
I unleashed whirlpools and undertows,
practicing, perfecting every motion.

I'd forgotten about it. But that's been me,
regular as tides, riding this train—
another little oblong world—till now.

What I have to perfect is how to calm this sea
the way I'd tilt the bottle, gently, slowly,
to counter the currents, until the storm passed
and the sky and water declared a truce.

Look, Annie, JUST TRY! Picture us,
you and me, maybe the summer before

I start college and you end suffering on Earth,
traveling cross-country on the train.
(Probably not the B&O, by then.)
Or . . . we can borrow someone's VW bus,
the kind with room to sleep where seats had been
so the Homers can have the head-out-the-window
vacation that Everydog dreams about.
You pick the cities . . . I'd be happy going
anywhere because happy isn't
about "where." No, it's got to be *here*,
wherever you are, right in front of your eyes.

Love from your brother in training,

> Perry

Niobrara County Library
Lusk, Wyoming 82225

A Note from the Author

Running with Trains is a work of fiction. A novel. But it's composed in poetry, which is classified as *nonfiction* at the library. And to further its multifaceted nature (I hope that's not the same thing as "confusing"), among its poetic forms are prose poems. (More on those in a moment.)

The interweaving poems of Perry and Steve were wholly invented by me (fiction) . . . even if it's true (the territory of nonfiction!) that I *have* lived parts of both boys' lives: For almost two decades, I've resided on an Ohio farm very much like the one on which Steve's family raises cattle. And, during the dizzying years as the 1960s turned into the 1970s, I was Perry's age, and resided in a major city in Ohio. (Columbus, rather than Cincinnati.) It's also true that in each of these locations—rural and urban—a part of me longed for the other.

But these two imagined lives *do* take place on or near an actual train, the *Cincinnatian*. It traveled one particular part of America in the year before privately owned, for-profit railways ceased operation as the federal government launched its intercity passenger train service, Amtrak, on May 1, 1971. My intention was to ground this book in *that* turbulent era, *that* Ohio terrain, and *that* struggling railroad line, but *simultaneously* to allow Steve and Perry's worlds to take flight—first in my imagination and then, assuming I'm successful, in yours.

Through interviews, photograph research, and archival documents, I gathered details such as the train numbers, the names of each station on the *Cincinnatian*'s route, the descriptions of the coach car's interior. But for specifics such as the actual arrival times at each station, or the kinds of food or baggage options offered during this book's time frame, my sources only referred to a range of years rather than to this precise year; they described the B&O Railroad, but not the *Cincinnatian* in particular. I trust that any minor deviations still allow this book to remain true to the experience of the era's train travel.

As for the poetry itself, I employed a range of forms to embody the voices of the two speakers. Much of the book is cast in blank verse, a poetic form that is composed of unrhymed, iambic pentameter lines.

(That's not as intimidating as it sounds! A line written in pentameter has five feet or beats. "Iambic" is a rhythm that's built of iams, and an iam is simply a word or phrase comprised of an unstressed syllable followed by a stressed syllable. For example: *these words / that fol/low in / ital/ics have / that rhy/thm—can / you hear / it now?* Blank verse has the tempo of a train. The pace of a heartbeat. *And much of human speech naturally falls into iambic cadence; like this line as well.*)

Blank verse provides other vital services, too. Each line

can be self-sufficient, holding one part of a sentence or one unit of thought. Each line can gather vowel sounds and consonants within its measures. Robert Frost called this a "sentence sound": It binds the words the way a clothesline arranges articles of clothing.

The momentum of iambic pentameter is also strong enough that I could sometimes alter it, substituting other metrical feet for iams, to give each boy's speech a colloquial, individual character. This more relaxed meter also keeps the poems from sounding too sing-song or predictable.

But other moments of the novel begged for shorter line lengths, rhyming patterns, or particular stanzaic groupings. Let me offer a few examples of why I chose or invented the form for a given poem.

In "Tickets," two- and four-beat lines alternate. Visually, as well as aurally, that emphasizes the chugging of the train, the beating of Steve's feet and heart. The shorter and longer measures likewise call to mind the alternating "lines" of wooden ties and gravel gaps along the tracks.

The rhyming quatrains (four-line stanzas) of "Between Stations" hints at the repeating patterns of a sermon, or the shifting back and forth between the two churches in Perry's mind. The echoing rhymes parallel the plot as well: Perry jots down the Wayside's sayings in his notebook precisely as the minister pens them . . . as Perry's train passes.

"How Can Something Be True If Its Opposite Is Also True?"

is a prose poem. Just as Perry numbers and lists his thoughts to keep them from spinning, I looked to the prose poem to capture something of this time period's uproar, protests, uneasiness. Indeed, the prose poem enjoyed a resurgence during this era of breaking traditions and pushing for new freedoms.

As a final example, "Snow Drafts," another prose poem, is something of a concrete poem: The arrangement of the words on the page suggests a shape. In this case, their rectangle is a simple sheet of paper, a regular expanse of snow that Steve might see through a window pane.

My first drafts of a poem help identify the form that is waiting to emerge. If I can find a few phrases, a line that truly works, I use it like a model or guide to orient the rest of the composition. Any form helps you argue with yourself. It's a self-imposed act of revision. It presents a challenge to each word, line, and idea you put to paper.

So I work to find the form that not only best presents the content, but also challenges and supports me as I move from wondering where on earth I am going, to welcoming whatever I've discovered.

Likewise, I hope that as you read these intertwining stories you experienced a similar journey . . . from wondering to welcoming.

—*MJR*

Hopewell Springs, Glenford, Ohio
November 2011

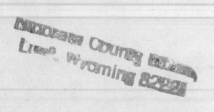

Niobrara County Library
Lusk, Wyoming 82225